PENGUIN BOOKS
NEGLECTED POEMS

One of the country's leading poets, Gulzar has published a number of poetry anthologies and collections of short stories. He is also regarded as one of India's finest writers for children. Apart from many Filmfare and National Awards for his films and lyrics—and an Oscar and Grammy for the song *Jai ho*—Gulzar has received the Sahitya Akademi Award in 2002 and the Padma Bhushan in 2004. He lives and works in Mumbai.

Pavan K. Varma is a writer and diplomat. His books include *The Great Indian Middle Class*, *Being Indian* and *Becoming Indian*, all published by Penguin. Apart from Gulzar's *Selected Poems*, he has translated Kaifi Azmi's and Atal Bihari Vajpayee's poetry into English for Penguin.

By the same author

Selected Poems, translated by Pavan K. Varma
100 Lyrics, translated by Sunjoy Shekhar

Neglected Poems

Gulzar

Translated by Pavan K. Varma

PENGUIN BOOKS

An imprint of Penguin Random House

PENGUIN BOOKS

USA | Canada | UK | Ireland | Australia
New Zealand | India | South Africa | China | Singapore

Penguin Books is part of the Penguin Random House group of companies
whose addresses can be found at global.penguinrandomhouse.com

Published by Penguin Random House India Pvt. Ltd
4th Floor, Capital Tower 1, MG Road,
Gurugram 122 002, Haryana, India

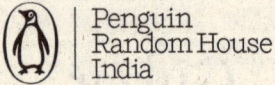

Penguin
Random House
India

First published in Viking by Penguin books India 2012

Published in Penguin books 2013

10 9 8 7 6 5 4 3 2

ISBN 9780143420293

Typeset in bembo by Eleven Arts, New Delhi
Printed at Repro India Limited

www.penguin.co.in

To Samay

Contents

Introduction

I share a lot of things with Pavan ji, and feel honoured that he allows me to share his evenings over a drink, over a poem or over a musical performance at home. What I enjoy the most about Pavan ji is his sense of humour, which always shines through his conversation.

On one such evening, I came up with a suggestion: There are so many collections called *Selected Poems*; why don't we name the new collection *Neglected Poems* instead?

Pavan ji looked acutely embarrassed. He started to explain that the delay in translating the new poems was because of his change of office and designation (he used to be Director of the ICCR in Delhi and now was India's Ambassador to Bhutan) . . . he hadn't meant to neglect the poems but somehow . . . Suddenly he saw a smile on my face and realized that I was only joking.

There is a saying that goes: 'You can miss a friend but you must not miss a joke'. So like two good friends we have stuck to the joke as far as the title of this book goes. It is now time to share the joke with everyone. Here they are then: the Neglected Poems.

Mumbai
December 2011

मेघना

समन्दर देख रहा था,
समन्दर से, मेरी अमृत की कुम्भी आने वाली थी
समन्दर करवटें लेता था, रह रह कर, तो बल पड़ते थे पानी में
मेरी बच्ची की नाज़ुक कोख से टीसें गुज़रती थीं
मुझे उस वक़्त डर लगता था 'अमृत' मांगने से

उसे जब कपकपी आती थी तो मैं कांप जाता था
वो प्यासी थी—
    मगर पानी मना था, बर्फ़ की डलियां फिराई जा रही थीं
      खुश्क होंठों पर

समन्दर अपने पानी में ही ग़ोते खाने लगता था
समन्दर काट के 'कुम्भी' निकालो
न काटोगे तो मर जायेगी बच्ची

मेरे 'अमृत की कुम्भी' को वो जब गोदी में लेकर अब खिलाती है
मेरे अन्दर से कोई मर्द कहता है
'तुम्हें तौफ़ीक़ ही न थी,
    कि तुम ये दर्द सहते, और इक इन्सान की तख़्लीक़ करते!!

Meghna (The Birth of Samay)

The ocean I was watching
From the ocean my pot of nectar was to come
Every time the ocean turned the waters would quiver
Throbbing pain would pass through
The fragile womb of my daughter
I would be afraid at that moment
To ask for my pot of nectar.

Whenever she would shudder, I would tremble
She was thirsty . . .
But water was not allowed
Cubes of ice were passed over her parched lips.

The ocean was going to convulse in its own waters
Slash the ocean and take out the pot
If you don't the mother will die!

Now, when she plays with my 'pot of nectar' on her lap
The male within me says:
'You never had the divine power
To bear this agony
And shoulder the pain of creating a human being!'

ख़्याल को वजूद देके, उसको ढूंढ़ते रहे!

ख़्याल को वजूद देके, उसको ढूंढ़ते रहे!
वजूद जो ख़्याल था!
दुआएं फूंकते रहे, धुएं में हम
कि आग की लपट उठे तो थाम लें
उसे तुम्हारा नाम दें।

पहाड़ों की गुफाओं में . . .
किसी ने जुस्तजू जला के रक्खी थी
और इन्तेज़ार के लिये,
समय की इन्तेहा हटा के रक्खी थी
इबादतें तराशे पत्थरों पे और घर बना लिये ख़्याल की पनाह के
      लिये
बस इक उम्मीद के गुनाह के लिये।

तमाम शब जली है शमा हिज्र की . . . .
उम्मीद भी बची है तो बस इतनी
जितनी एक बांझ की कोख को उम्मीद हो!!

In Search, Giving Form to Thought

Searching for Him
By giving form to thought;
That form which is no more than thought.
Prodding alive the fire of prayer and
Waiting, amidst the smoke,
For that leap of flame
Which I can hold
And call by your name.

Deep inside the womb of mountains
Someone had kept the flame of desire alive
And set no limits
To the time for waiting.
Worship was honed against unyielding stone
And shelters built to give refuge to thought,
Just to keep alive the possibility of hope.

All night the fire of separation has burnt . . .
If any hope is left it is only
Like the yearning
Of a barren woman for a womb!

ठीक से याद नहीं . . .

ठीक से याद नहीं,
फ़्रांस में 'बोर्दो' के पास कहीं
थोड़ी सी देर रूके थे
छोटे से क़सबे में, इक छोटा सा लकड़ी का गिरजा
सामने 'ऑलटर' के, बेंच थी . . .
एक ही शायद

भेड़ उठाये हुये इक 'ईसा' की चोबी मूरत
लोगों की शम'ओं से
पांव कुछ झुलसे हुये
पिघली हुई मोम में कुछ डूबे हुये
जिस्म पर मेख़ें लगी थीं
एक कन्धे पे थी, जोड़ जहां खुलने लगा था
एक निकली हुई पहलू से जिसे भेड़ की टांग में ठोक दिया था
एक कोहनी के ज़रा नीचे जहां टूट गई थी लकड़ी . . .
गिर के शायद . . . या सफ़ाई करते!

I Cannot Remember Clearly

I cannot remember clearly,
In France somewhere near Bordeaux
We stopped for a while.
In a small village a small wooden church,
A bench before the altar,
Just one perhaps.

Holding a lamb
A wooden image of Jesus:
The feet slightly blackened
By the candles lit by people
Looking a bit drowned in the melting wax.
On his body nails:
One on his shoulder, where the joint had begun to cleave;
Another protruding from under the garment
Onto which the leg of the lamb was hammered;
One just below the elbow
Where a piece of wood had broken;
On its own perhaps
Or while cleaning.

कभी आना पहाड़ों पर . . .

कभी आना पहाड़ों पर . . .
धुली बर्फ़ों के नम्दे डाल कर आसन बिछाये हैं
पहाड़ों की ढलानों पर बहुत से जंगलों के ख़ेमे खींचे हैं
तनाबें बांध रखी हैं कई देवदार के मज़बूत पेड़ों से
पलाश और गुलमोहर के, हाथों से काढ़े हुये तकिये लगाये हैं
तुम्हारे रास्तों पर छांव छिड़की है
मैं बादल धुनता रहता हूं
कि गहरी वादियां ख़ाली नहीं होतीं
ये चिल्मन बारिशों की भी उठा दूंगा, जब आओगे

मुझे तुम ने ज़मीं दी थी
तुम्हारे रहने के क़ाबिल यहां इक घर बना दूं मैं
कभी फ़ुर्सत मिले जब बाक़ी कामों से तो आ जाना
किसी 'वीक एन्ड' पे आ जाओ!

Come Sometime to the Mountains

Come sometime to the mountains
Rugs of washed snow are spread out for you
The forests on the slopes have erected tents
Tethered to the ground by strong deodar trees
Hand-embroidered pillows of palash and gulmohar are
    arrayed
Shade is sprinkled on the roads your feet will tread.
I keep carding clouds
So that the deep valleys do not look empty;
I will even lift the veil of the falling rain
When you come.

You gave me the earth
On which I could build
A home good enough for you to live;
Come, when you find time from all your other chores
Maybe on some 'weekend', come!

दोनों इक सड़क के आर—पार चल रहे हैं हम

दोनों इक सड़क के आर—पार चल रहे हैं हम
उस तरफ़ से उसने कुछ कहा जो मुझ तक आते—आते
    रास्ते के शोरो—गुल में खो गया . . .
मैंने कुछ इशारे से कहा मगर
चलते—चलते दोनों की नज़र न मिल सकी

उसे मुग़ालता है मैं
उसी की जुस्तजू में हूं
मुझे ये शक है, वो कहीं
वो न हो, जो मुझ से छुपता फिरता है!

We Are Both Walking on Either Side
of the Road

Both of us are walking on two sides of the same road:
From the other side He said something
Which was lost in the noise by the time it reached me;
I signaled to Him, to say something
But we were walking, our eyes did not meet.

He is under the illusion
That I am still searching for Him
I have this doubt that He may be the one
Who seeks to hide from me!

सर्दी थी और कोहरा था . . . .

सर्दी थी और कोहरा था और सुबह की बस आधी आंख खुली थी,
    आधी नींद में थी!
शिमला से जब नीचे आते
एक पहाड़ी के कोने में
बस्ते जितनी बस्ती भी इक
बटवे जितना मन्दिर था
साथ लगी मस्जिद, वो भी लॉकेट जितनी
नींद भरी दो बाहों जैसे मस्जिद के मीनार गले में मन्दिर के,
दो मासूम खुदा सोये थे!
इक बूढ़े झरने के नीचे!!

It Was Cold and Misty

It was cold and misty
The morning's eye, still not fully awake,
Was half shut, half open.
On the way down from Simla
In one corner of a mountain
A settlement the size of a suitcase
A temple the size of a wallet
And a mosque adjacent, that too not bigger than a locket.
Like two arms immersed in sleep
The mosque's minarets embraced the temple.

Two innocent gods fast asleep
Below an ancient spring.

बारिश होती है जब . . .

बारिश होती है जब . . .
तो इन गारे पत्थर की दीवारों पर
भीगे–भीगे नक़्शे बनने लगते हैं
हिचकी–हिचकी बारिश तब . . .
पहचानी सी एक लिखाई लिखती है
बारिश कुछ कह जाती है

ऐसा ही अश्कों से भीगा
इक ख़त शायद, तुमने पहले देखा हो?

When It Rains

When it rains
Drenched figures begin to emerge
On these mud and mortar walls;
Then the rain, falling gently, like muted hiccups,
Writes a familiar script:
The rain conveys something.

Perhaps you may recall having seen
A letter drenched in tears
That looked something like this?

बारिश आती है तो . . .

बारिश आती है तो मेरे शहर को कुछ हो जाता है
टीन की छत, तिरपाल का छज्जा, पीपल, पत्ते परनाला
   सब बजने लगते हैं

तंग गली में जाते—जाते
साईकिल का पहिया पानी की कुल्लियां करता है
बारिश में कुछ लम्बे हो जाते हैं क़द भी लोगों के
जितने ऊपर हैं, उतने ही पैरों के नीचे पानी में
ऊपर वाला तैरता है तो नीचे वाला डूब के चलता है

ख़ुश्क था तो रस्ते में टिक टिक छतरी टेक के चलते थे
बारिश में आकाश पे छतरी टेक के टप—टप चलते हैं!

When the Rain Comes

When the rains come something happens to my city:
Tin roofs, canvas awnings, peepul trees, leaves, drain
    pipes
All begin to resound.

The bicycle's wheel
Negotiating a narrow lane
Gurgles with the water;
People also seem a little taller
During the monsoons:
They are as much above as under the water
If one half-swims, the other walks below, drowned.

When it was dry we walked on the path
Using our umbrella, tick-tick, on the ground;
In the rains, resting our umbrella on the sky,
Tup-tup we go along!

मॉनसून की सिम्फ़नी

कार का इंजन बंद कर के
और शीशे चढ़ा के बारिश में
घने–घने पेड़ों से ढकी 'सेंट पॉल रोड' पर
आंखें मीच के बैठे रहो और कार की छत पर
        ताल सुनो तब बारिश की!

गीले बदन कुछ हवा के झोंके
पेड़ों की शाख़ों पर चलते दिखते हैं
शीशे पे फिसलते पानी की तहरीर में उंगलियां चलती हैं
कुछ ख़त, कुछ सतरें याद आती हैं
मॉनसून की सिम्फ़नी में!

The Monsoon Symphony

Under the densely green trees of St Paul's Road
Shut the engine of the car
Wind up the windows
Sit with your eyes closed
And then hear the rhythm of the rain
On the roof of your car.

See gusts of wind
Like drenched bodies
Walking on the branches of trees;
Your fingers tap
To the beat of the water's narrative
As it slips down your windshield;
Some letters, some lines from the past,
Come to mind
In this monsoon symphony!

बारिश आने से पहले ही . . .

बारिश आने से पहले ही
बारिश से बचने की तैयारी जारी है
सारी दरारें बन्द कर ली हैं
और लेप के छत, अब छतरी भी मढ़वा ली है
खिड़की जो खुलती है बाहर
उसके ऊपर भी इक छज्जा खींच दिया है
'मेन सड़क' से गली में होकर, दरवाज़े तक आता रस्ता
बजरी मिट्टी डाल के उसको कूट रहे हैं
यहीं कहीं कुछ गड्ढों में
बारिश आती है तो पानी भर जाता है
जूते, पांव, पांयचे सब सन जाते हैं

गले न पड़ जाए सतरंगी
भीग न जाएं बादल से
सावन से बच कर जीते हैं
बारिश आने से पहले
बारिश से बचने की तैयारी जारी है!!

Before the Rains Come

Before the rains come
Work has begun to escape them!
All crevices have been closed
The roof given a fresh coating
Even the umbrella repaired;
An awning has been put
On the window that opens outside;
Fresh gravel is being pounded on
The lane off the main road
Coming to the door of the house;
In ditches here and there
Water fills when the rains come
Soiling shoes, socks and feet.

Lest the rainbow wraps around us in an embrace
Or the clouds drench us
We live in fear of the monsoons;
Before the rains come
Work has begun to escape them!

पंखे से उड़ती है तो बल्ब पे जा बैठती है . . .

पंखे से उड़ती है तो बल्ब पे जा बैठती है . . .
आईना देखती है दो तरफ़ झटक कर गर्दन
इतनी सी चिड़िया है, कुल एक छटंकी भर की
जब चहकती है तो सर ही पे उठा लेती है सारा कमरा
ख़बरें भी ठीक से सुनने नहीं देती मुझ को

कितने मासूमों के घर दंगों में जल कर
मलबे का ढेर हुये जाते हैं गुजरात में . . .
. . . और ये है,
एक टूटे हुये रौज़न में इसे
तिनके सजाने की पड़ी है!

From the Fan She Flies to the Bulb

Flying off the fan
She finds a perch on the bulb;
Jerks her neck this side and that to look into the mirror;
Such a small sparrow, not more than a gram in all
But brings the house down with her chirping,
Does not even let me hear the news properly.

How many homes of innocents
Keep getting reduced to heaps of ash
In the riots of Gujarat . . .
And this bird
All she cares about is how to array twigs
In the broken skylight.

बग़दाद

जंग का कूड़ा एक जगह पर जमा हुआ है
पहली बार है . . .
इतने सारे बाजू, टांगें, हाथ और सर और पांव
    ऐसे अलग–अलग बिखरे देखे हैं
बचे–खुचे पुरज़े लगते हैं
'स्पेयर पार्ट्स' हैं

बाजू एक जुलाहे का, हिलता है अब तक
कांप रहा है या शायद कुछ कात रहा है
टांग है एक खिलाड़ी की . . . रन आउट हुआ है
घर तक दौड़ते–दौड़ते राह में मारा गया

सर है एक, जो लुढ़क रहा है
टूटे–फूटे शेर अभी तक सर में खड़–खड़ बजते हैं
नज़्मों के छंद टूट गये हैं
उंगलियां रेंग रही हैं कुछ
मिट्टी में तारीख़ दर्ज करने की कोशिश लगती है

पुरज़ा–पुरज़ा खोल के एक मैकेनिक ने
उनकी मरम्मत चाही थी . . .
बुरा लगा था उसको ये पुरज़े आवाज़ें करते हैं!!

24

Baghdad

The debris of war has collected at one place
For the first time . . . .
So many arms, legs, hands, heads and feet
Can be seen separately scattered about
Like 'spare parts'.

A weaver's arm still moves
Trembling, or perhaps still weaving
Here is the leg of a sportsman, run out,
Killed while he was running home.

There is a head, rolling around
Broken couplets still rumbling inside;
The verses of poems have come undone;
Fingers grovel about
Trying, it would seem, to inscribe
The date in the mud.

Opening each and every part
A mechanic wanted to repair them . . .
He was offended to find
That these parts still have a voice!

गुजरात

सारे बदन पर, पित निकली है
हाथ खुरचते हैं पैरों को
पैर मसलते हैं गर्दन
गर्दन फंसी हुई है सर में
सर में कैक्ट्स उगे हुए हैं
जहां–जहां मज़हब की बिच्छू बूटी छू ले
वहां–वहां ख़ारिश होती है
फोड़े फूटने लगते हैं
पीप निकलने लगती है!

Gujarat

A feverish rash has spread over the whole body:
The hands scratch the legs
The legs crush the neck
The neck is entangled with the head
And cacti grow from the skull.

Wherever the scorpio-nettle
Of religious strife touches
Scabs break out
Boils erupt
Pus begins to ooze!

इक पीपल था . . .

कहते हैं इक पीपल था
ऊपर वाली बर्फ़ की चोटी से उतरा था
कुन्डली मार के धूप में इक दरिया सोया था
उस पर पांव पड़ा और पीपल . . . ठहर गया
सूरज ने देखा, दरिया की आंख में पीपल की तस्वीर उतर आई थी
दरिया दिन भर गुन–गुन करता रहता था
रात को करवट लेकर, पीपल के ज़ानू पर सर रख कर सोचा
     करता था
काश खड़ा हो सकता वो भी पैरों पर
और गले लग सकता उठ कर पीपल के
इक सिंदूरी शाम कमर लहराती हुई
दोनों के बीच से हो कर रोज़ निकलती थी

जब कुछ सदियां बीत गईं
और आसमान के बाल भी कनपटियों के नीचे पकने लगे
एक रोज़ उस चिकनी शाम का हाथ पकड़ कर पीपल ने रोका
     उसको . . . सुन
क्यों मुंह काला करने जाती है तू रोज़ उसी सूरज के
     पीछे–पीछे . . . पार उफ़क़ के?

लाली फिर गई शाम के मुंह पर
शाख़ से पत्ता तोड़ के
लिख कर चिट्ठी उस पर,
हाथ में दी . . . जा, जा कर देना उस आकाश स्वामी को।

Once There Was a Peepal

They say there was once a peepal
It had descended from the snow-capped pinnacle above
A river coiled under the sun was asleep
The peepal stepped on it . . . and stopped.
The sun saw the peepal's image was in the river's eye
The whole day the river would hum
At night, turning on its side and putting its head on the
    peepal's knees,
It would think:
If only I too could stand up on my feet
And embrace this peepal tree!
A crimson dusk swaying its hips
Would pass every day between the two.

When a few centuries passed
And the sky's hair too began to grey below the temples
One day the peepal caught the hand of that saucy dusk:
Why do you go running across the sky
To that same sun every day
To blacken your name?

A red tinge suffused the dusk's face
The peepal wrote a letter
On a leaf plucked from a branch
And put it in her hand:
Go! Go give this to the lord of the skies!

शाम का चेहरा स्याह होते–होते वो भागी
लेकिन राह में . . .
चांद ने हाथ मरोड़ के चिट्ठी छीन ली उससे
राहु, केतु, भागे हाथ छुड़ाने उसका
शाम का कंगन सटका हाथ से, और शनि ने दौड़ के कंगन लूट
    लिया
बड़बोला 'दुमदार सितारा' महवर–महवर शोर मचाता भाग गया
सदियों तक गूंजी थी फिर वो बात घुमड़ती कायनात में

सदियों बाद की बात है शायद . . .
या फिर उन्हीं दिनों की होगी
वक़्त खड़ाऊं पहने, जब कुछ सय्यारों पर पांव रखता
    कायनात से गुज़र रहा था . . .

पीपल का इक पत्ता उड़ते–उड़ते
उसकी पीठ से आकर चिपक गया
वक़्त ने अपना रुख़ बदला और . . .
पर्बत–पर्बत पांव रखता नीचे उतरा
रात की गोद में शाम पड़ी थी
दरिया लिपटा हुआ खड़ा था पीपल से
और पहाड़ के सीने पर, पहली–पहली घास उगी थी!

Before her face blanched to ash
The dusk ran . . .
But on the way the moon twisted her wrist
And snatched the letter
Rahu, Ketu ran to free her hand
Her bracelet slipped off
And was grabbed by Saturn
The garrulous Haley's Comet went from orbit to orbit
Spreading the news
For centuries the incident reverberated in the cosmos.

Many centuries later perhaps . . .
Or maybe just then
When Time, stepping over galaxies in wooden clogs,
Was traversing the cosmos
A peepal leaf wafting by
Stuck to its back
And Time changed its course . . .

Climbing down the mountains
It descended
The dusk was lying in the lap of the night
The river was standing entwined with the peepal
And on the mountain's chest the very first grass had
    sprouted!

इक नक़ल तुझे भी भेजूंगा . . .

इक नक़ल तुझे भी भेजूंगा
ये सोच के ही . . .
तन्हाई के नीचे कार्बन पेपर रखके मैं
ऊंची–ऊंची आवाज़ में बातें करता हूं

अल्फ़ाज़ उतर आते हैं काग़ज़ पर लेकिन . . .
आवाज़ की शक्ल उतरती नहीं
रातों की सियाही दिखती है!!

I Will Give You a Copy Too

Only because I think
That I will send you a copy too
I keep a carbon paper below my loneliness
And talk loudly all the while.

My words are reproduced on the paper
But not the feel of my voice
At night I only see the ink-like darkness.

सैकड़ों बार गिने थे मैंने . . .

सैकड़ों बार गिने थे मैंने
जेब में नौ ही कंचे थे
एक जेब से दूसरी जेब में रखते–रखते
इक कंचा खो बैठा हूं
न हारा, न गिरा कहीं पर
'प्लूटो' मेरे आसमान से ग़ायब है!!

I Had Counted a Hundred Times

I had counted a hundred times:
There were only nine marbles.
Putting them from one pocket to the other
I have gone and mislaid one!
Not lost in a game, nor dropped somewhere:
Pluto has just disappeared from my sky!

मटका भर के सूरज उल्टा . . .

मटका भर के सूरज उल्टा, शाम ने दूर समन्दर की दहलीज़ पे
    जाकर
रात का पशमीना पहने तुम आई थीं!

रात तुम्हारे जिस्म से फिसली पड़ती थी
जिस्म तुम्हारा इक जलते सय्यारे सा
दूध और धूप से गूंधी मिट्टी
एक फ़लक भर खुश्बू थी आवाज़ तुम्हारी

तुम बोल रही थीं
होंठ तुम्हारे चांद की क़ाशें काट रहे थे
मैं हैरां . . .
हैरां हैरां . . .
मटका भर के सूरज का, एक और सहर निकली पानी से
उंगली थाम के सुबह की तुम पानी पर चलते–चलते एक और
उफ़क़ को लौट गईं

वक़्त के पुरइसरार किसी 'कौमेट' की तरह
कायनात से आईं तुम और कायनात में लौट गईं!!

Like a Pot Brimful the Sun Upturned

At dusk, far in the horizon, on the ocean's threshold,
The sun's brimful pot upturned:
You came draped in the night's pashmina shawl.

The night kept slipping all over your body
Your body was like an incandescent planet
Mud kneaded with milk and sunshine
Your voice a fragrance pervading the sky.

You were speaking
Your lips chiseling the pieces of the moon
And I was wondering . . .
Wondering, wondering.

One more dawn
With a pot brimful of sun
Emerged in the distant water
While you
Holding the dawn's finger
Walked across the water
Returning to yet another horizon.

Like some comet hidden in the mystery of time,
You came from the cosmos and returned to it!

धूप का पुरज़ा . . .

शाम का सूरज जाते–जाते
दरवाज़े के नीचे से
धूप का इक छोटा सा पुरज़ा फेंक गया है
कल आऊं निश्चित तो नहीं है
लेकिन इस मामूरे में
आज का दिन भी जी पाये तुम
इसी लिये . . .
ये पर्ची रख जाता हूं कि सनद रहे!

A Piece of the Sun

The sun as it sets
Has flung from under the door
A small chit of sunshine:
Whether I return tomorrow is not certain
But if you have managed
In this waste-yard
To live for this one day more
I leave behind this chit
As testament.

चिट्टे दूधिया बादलों में इक भेड़ का बच्चा

चिट्टे दूधिया बादलों में इक भेड़ का बच्चा
अंधाधुंद ही, प्लेन के पीछे भाग रहा था
बायें विंग से टकराया है
ज़ख़्मी होकर लुढ़क गया है
सूरज लौट रहा था, उसने रुक कर देखा
      और कुछ पल को ठहर गया . . .
रूई के गालों से उसने कोशिश की है पोंछने की
पर खून अभी तक रुका नहीं है
पूरे उफ़क़ पर फैल रहा है!!

A Lamb Among White Milky Clouds

Amidst white, milky clouds
A lamb was blindly running after a plane;
The left wing struck it:
Wounded, it has staggered to one side.
The sun was returning; it stopped to see
And paused for a moment;
It tried to wipe off the blood with cotton buds
But the blood has not yet stemmed:
It is spreading over the entire horizon!

दो परिन्दे . . .

टुकड़ा इक धूप का जिस खिड़की से आया था, उसी खिड़की
से वापस जाकर
कांच पे ठहर गया . . .
मुड़ के फिर जायज़ा कमरे का लिया
और आहिस्ता से जाकर
लॉन में सहमे हुए एक परिन्दे की तरह बैठ गया

इक झपट्टे ही में, शाम उसको उठा कर
आम के पेड़ पे जा बैठी, उसे नोच दिया
बालो—पर धूप के उस पेड़ से फिर, देर तलक गिरते रहे!!

Two Birds

Returning from the very window it came in
A piece of the sun
Paused on the glass-pane
Turned around to inspect the room
And then quietly
Went and sat on the lawn like a frightened bird.

In one fell swoop the dusk snatched it away
Took it to the branch of a mango tree
And shredded it;
The feathers and pieces of the sun
Kept falling from that tree
For very long!

तेरे उतारे हुए दिन टंगे हैं लॉन में अब तक . . .

तेरे उतारे हुए दिन टंगे हैं लॉन में अब तक
न वो पुराने हुए हैं, न उनका रंग उतरा
कहीं से कोई भी सीवन अभी नहीं उधड़ी

इलायची के बहुत पास रखे पत्थर पर
ज़रा सी जलदी सरक आया करती है छांव
ज़रा सा और घना हो गया है वो पौदा
मैं थोड़ा–थोड़ा वो गमला हटाता रहता हूं–
फ़क़ीरा अब भी वहीं मेरी कॉफ़ी देता है

गिलहरियों को बुला कर खिलाता हूं बिस्किट
गिलहरियां मुझे शक की नज़र से देखती हैं
वो तेरे हाथों का मस जानती होंगी

कभी–कभी जब उतरती है चील शाम की छत से
थकी–थकी सी ज़रा देर लॉन में रुक कर
सफ़ेद और गुलाबी, 'मसुंडे' के पौदों में घुलने लगती है
कि जैसे बर्फ़ का टुकड़ा पिघलता जाये व्हिस्की में
मैं 'स्कार्फ़' दिन का गले से उतार देता हूं
तेरे उतारे हुए दिन पहन के अब भी मैं
तेरी महक में कई रोज़ काट देता हूं!!

The Days You Discarded . . .

The days you discarded are still hung in the lawn
They do not look old, nor have they faded
Not even a crease has come apart.

On the stone right next to the cardamom bush
The shadow creeps up a bit earlier
The plant has become a little greener
I keep moving the flower pot slightly
Faqira still serves me my coffee there.

I invite squirrels and give them biscuits
They look at me with suspicion
Perhaps, they know the scent of your hands.

Sometimes when the evening kite descends from the roof
A bit tired, resting a while on the lawn
It begins to dissolve in the white and pink *masanda*
Like a piece of ice in a whisky tumbler
I take off the scarf of the day from my neck.
Wearing the days you discarded
I spend many a day lost in your fragrance.

मुझे अफ़सोस है सोना . . .

मुझे अफ़सोस है सोना . . .
कि मेरी नज़्म से होकर गुज़रते वक़्त बारिश में,
    परेशानी हुई तुम को . . .
बड़े बे–वक़्त आते हैं यहां सावन,
मेरी नज़्मों की गलियां यूं भी अक्सर भीगी रहती हैं
कई गड्ढों में पानी जमा रहता है
अगर पांव पड़े तो मोच आ जाने का ख़तरा है

मुझे अफ़सोस है लेकिन . . .
परेशानी हुई तुमको कि मेरी नज़्म में कुछ रौशनी कम है
गुज़रते वक़्त दहलीज़ों के पत्थर भी नहीं दिखते
कि मेरे पैरों के नाखून कितनी बार टूटे हैं . . .
हुई मुद्दत कि चौराहे पे अब बिजली का खम्बा भी नहीं जलता
परेशानी हुई तुम को . . .
मुझे अफ़सोस है सचमुच!!

I Am Sorry, Sona

I am sorry, Sona . . .
Passing by my poem in the rain
Must have been troublesome for you . . .

The monsoons here always come at the wrong time
In any case, the alleyways of my poems are often
    drenched
So many potholes remain filled with water
If you step into one of them your foot can get sprained.

I am sorry
It must have distressed you that my poem is not well lit
Even the stones in the threshold are not visible as you
    pass by
So many times the nails of my foot have broken
For ages now the lamppost at the crossing has not
    worked
It must have discomfited you
I am sorry, Sona, really I am!

वक़्त को जितना गूंध सके हम . . .

वक़्त को जितना गूंध सके हम, गूंध लिया
आटे की मिक़दार कभी बढ़ भी जाती है
भूख मगर इक हद से आगे बढ़ती नहीं
पेट के मारों की ऐसी ही आदत है . . .
भर जाये तो दस्तरख़्वान से उठ जाते हैं

आओ, अब उठ जायें दोनों
कोई कचहरी का खूंटा दो इन्सानों को
दस्तरख़्वान पे कब तक बांध के रख सकता है
क़ानूनी मोहरों से कब रुकते हैं, या कटते हैं रिश्ते
रिश्ते राशन कार्ड नहीं हैं!!

We Have Kneaded Time Enough

As much as we could knead time, we have!
The dough may sometimes increase in bulk
But hunger cannot cross a certain line
The hungry have this habit:
Once full, they get up and leave the feast!

Come, let us both get up
No court can bind two people
To sit forever at the table;
Since when have legal seals
Held back or broken a relationship?
Relationships are not a ration card!

मैं क़ैदी हूं . . .

कई पिंजरों का क़ैदी हूं . . .
कई पिंजरों में बसता हूं
मुझे भाता है क़ैदें काटना
        और अपनी मरज़ी से चुनाव करते रहना
        अपने पिंजरों का . . .
मीयादें तय नहीं करता मैं रिश्तों की
असीरी ढूंढ़ता हूं मैं
असीरी अच्छी लगती है!!

I Am a Prisoner

I am a prisoner of many cages
I live in many cages
I like to be incarcerated
And to keep on choosing, by my own sweet will,
My various prisons . . .
I do not fix the length of my relationships
I seek imprisonment
I like to be a captive.

ट्रैफ़िक सिगनल . . .

होंठ हिलते हैं भिखारी के, सुनाई नहीं देता
हाथ के लफ़्ज़ उछलते हैं, वो कुछ बोल रहा है
थपथपाता है हर इक कार का शीशा आकर
और उजलत में है
ट्रैफ़िक के सिगनल पे नज़र है!

'चेंज' है तो सही
कौन इस गर्मी में अब कार का शीशा खोले
अगले सिगनल पे सही
रोज़ कुछ देना ज़रूरी है, ख़ुदा राज़ी रहे!

Traffic Signal

The beggar's lips move, but can't be heard
Words, formed by hands, spring up
Indicating that something is being said.
He taps the panes of every car
And is in a hurry
His eyes are on the traffic signal.

I have some change
But in this heat who wants to open the window
At the next signal then . . .
God be pleased, something must be donated every day!

पूर्ण सूरज ग्रहण . . .

कॉलेज के रोमांस में ऐसा होता था
डेस्क के पीछे बैठे–बैठे
चुपके से दो हाथ सरकते
धीरे–धीरे पास आते . . .
और फिर एक, अचानक पूरा हाथ पकड़ लेता था
मुट्ठी में भर लेता था
सूरज ने यूंही पकड़ा है चांद का हाथ फ़लक में आज!!

Total Solar Eclipse

In college romances it used to happen so:
From behind a desk two hands
Would furtively, slowly, begin to slide towards each
    other . . .
And then suddenly, one would completely hold the
    other
Cover it fully by the palm;
Today the sun has caught the hand of the moon
Just like that.

दरिया—ए—ब्यास जहां बहता है . . .

दरिया—ए—ब्यास जहां बहता है
उससे थोड़ी दूरी पर
पन्द्रह—बीस घरों की एक पहाड़ी बस्ती के सिरहाने
आलती—पालती मारे बैठा
सूखा गंजा एक पहाड़ . . .
दिन में कितने सारे रूप बदलता है

सुबह सात या आठ बजे
सूरज की इक परछाई, कुछ यूं पड़ती है आकर उसके माथे पर,
जैसे एक तिलकधारी साधु है, जो पद्मासन में, ध्यान लगाये बैठा है,
नीचे की तरफ़ चट्टान का ख़म
तुड्डी के बीचों बीच पड़ा, हड्डी का दबाव लगता है

कभी—कभी 'सेलर' लगता है
बदली का मफ़लर पहने
'डेक' पर आकर ग़ौर से देख रहा है कितनी दूर उफ़क़ है
ऊपर के दोनों पत्थर उस धूप में 'गॉगल्ज़' लगते हैं

धूप ढले फिर यूं लगता है
'बुलडॉग' कोई नथनों को फुलाये बैठा है
चौकन्ना है . . .
दरिया ने अगर बस्ती की तरफ़ कुछ रेंगने की कोशिश की तो
गुर्रा कर उस पर झपटेगा

Where the Beas Flows

Not far from where the Beas flows
Near a village of some fifteen-twenty homes
Sits cross-legged
A barren and bald mountain
Changing countless forms during the day.

In the morning, around seven or eight,
The sun's shadow falls in such a way on its forehead
As though a sadhu with a tilak on his forehead
Is sitting in padma asan in meditation
The bend of the cliff dropping below
Is like a bone pressing squarely against the chin.

Sometimes it looks like a sailor
Wearing the clouds as a scarf
Coming up to the deck, intently gauging the limits of
    the horizon,
The two rocks above like goggles in the glare.

When the sun sets
It looks like a bulldog with its nostrils flared up
All alert
If the river makes any attempt to slink towards the village
It would attack, growling!

पन्द्रह–बीस घरों की एक पहाड़ी बस्ती के सिरहाने
आलती–पालती मारे बैठा
सूखा गंजा एक पहाड़
दिन में कितने सारे रूप बदलता है!!

Near a village of some fifteen-twenty homes
Sits cross-legged
A barren and bald mountain
Changing countless forms during the day!

अच्छे लगते हैं ये पहाड़ मुझे

अच्छे लगते हैं ये पहाड़ मुझे
चोटियां बादलों में उड़ती हैं
पांव बर्फ़ाब बहते पानी में
कूटते रहते हैं नदियां
कितनी संजीदगी से जीते हैं
किस क़दर मुस्तक़िल–मिज़ाज हैं ये
अच्छे लगते हैं ये पहाड़ मुझे!!

These Mountains, I Like Them

I like these mountains . . .
Peaks flying in the clouds
Feet pounding away at the
Ice-cold waters of rivers flowing below
How wisely they live
With such stable, unchanging temperaments.
I like these mountains!

रोहतांग के नीचे . . .

रोहतांग के नीचे
कोहरे में लिपटी सिमटी इक वादी को
सारा साल ही नज़ला रहता है

बर्फ़ पड़े तो जम जाता है
धूप पड़े तो फिर से बहने लगता है
सारा साल मगर उसको हलका सा रेशा रहता है

पत झड़ में भी छींकों की इक झड़ी लगी ही रहती है
छींटे उड़ते रहते हैं
सुड़क—सुड़क करती रहती है
सारा साल ही इस वादी को
नज़ला रहता है!!

Below the Rohtang

Below the Rohtang
A valley withdrawn, wrapped in mist,
Has a bad cold all the year long.

When it snows the cold congeals
When the sun is out it begins to flow
But throughout the year a slight congestion is there.

In autumn too, a string of sneezes
Drop here, there, in the air
'Suduk, suduk' it sniffles along
All the year long
This valley has a bad cold.

रात पहाड़ों पर कुछ और ही होती है

रात पहाड़ों पर कुछ और ही होती है
आसमान बुझता ही नहीं
और दरिया रौशन रहता है
इतना ज़री का काम नज़र आता है फ़लक पे तारों का
जैसे रात में 'प्लेन' से रौशन शहर दिखाई देते हैं

पास ही दरिया आंख पे काली पट्टी बांध के
पेड़ों के झुरमट में–
कोड़ा जमाल शाही, 'आई जुमेरात आई . . . पीछे देखे शामत
   आई . . .'
दौड़ दौड़ के खेलता है

कंघी रख के दांतों में
आवाज़ किया करती है हवा
कुछ फटी–फटी . . . झीनी–झीनी . . .
बालिग़ होते लड़कों की तरह

इतना ऊंचा–ऊंचा बोलते हैं दो झरने आपस में
जैसे एक देहात के दोस्त अचानक मिल कर वादी में
गांव भर का पूछते हों . . .
नज़्म भी आधी आंखें खोल के सोती है
रात पहाड़ों पर कुछ और ही होती है!!

Mountain Night

The night in the mountains is something else:
The sky never darkens
And the river is forever alight
So much zari work can be seen
In the sky through the pattern of the stars:
Just like a city looks
All lit from a plane at night.

The wind speaks like someone
Holding a comb between the teeth
Cracking a little, a trifle threadbare
Like that of a boy coming of age.

Two waterfalls speak so loudly to each other
Like rustic friends
Meeting unexpectedly in a valley
Discussing the entire village;
Even a poem sleeps with its eyes half-open:
The night in the mountains is something else.

जब भी उतरोगे तुम पहाड़ों से

जब भी उतरोगे तुम पहाड़ों से
नीचे बहते ब्यास के कंडे
एक पत्थर मिलेगा पानी में
जी करे तो उठा के रख लेना
टूट कर मैं गिरा था चोटी से!

Whenever You Come Down from
the Mountains

Whenever you come down from the mountains
You will find a pebble
In a pool of the flowing Beas.
If you feel like, pick it up,
Broken, I had fallen from the peak above.

मद्रास (चेन्नई)

शहर ये बुजुर्ग लगता है
फैलने लगा है अब
जैसे बूढ़े लोगों का पेट बढ़ने लगता है
जुबां के ज़ायक़े वही
लिबास के सलीक़े भी
पतली–पतली गलियां धीरे–धीरे चलती रहती हैं
और रगों में खून बहता रहता है
खुश्की बढ़ गई है जिस्म पर, 'कावेरी' सूखी रहती है
शाम को भी जल्द नींद आने लगती है इसे
बूढ़ा तो नहीं मगर . . .
शहर ये बुजुर्ग लगता है!

Chennai

This city looks elderly
It has begun to spread
Like the bellies of old people.
The same relish for language
The same good taste in dress
Its narrow lanes keep moving slowly
And blood keeps coursing through the veins.
The skin is drier, the Kaveri is mostly without water,
By evening the city is already yawning.
Not exactly old yet . . .
But this city looks elderly.

बंबई

बड़ी लम्बी सी मछली की तरह लेटी हुई पानी में ये नगरी
कि सर पानी में और पांव ज़मीं पर हैं
समन्दर छोड़ती है, न समन्दर में उतरती है
ये नगरी बंबई की . . .
जुराबें लम्बे लम्बे साहिलों की, पिंडलियों तक खींच रखी हैं
समन्दर खेलता रहता है पैरों से लिपट कर
हमेशा छींकता है, शाम होती है तो 'टाईड' में

यहीं देखा है साहिल पर
समन्दर, ओक में भर के
'जोशान्दे' की तरह हर रोज़ पी जाता है सूरज को
बड़ा तंदुरुस्त रहता है
कभी दुबला नहीं होता
कभी लगता है ये कोई तिलस्मी सा जज़ीरा है
जज़ीरा बम्बई का . . .

किसी गिरगिट की चमड़ी से बना है आसमां इसका
जो वादों की तरह रंगत बदलता है
'कसीनो' में रखे 'रोलेट' की सूरत चलता रहता है
कभी इस शहर की गर्दिश नहीं रुकती
इसे 'ब्येरिंग' लगे हैं
किसी 'एक्सेल' पे रक्खा है

Mumbai

Like a very long fish lying in water
Head immersed, feet on the land,
This city
Neither leaves the sea, nor enters it
This city of Mumbai . . .
Its seashores are like long socks
Pulled up to the calf
With the playful ocean at its feet.
This city always sneezes when the tide comes up at
    dusk.

Only here can you see
The sea at the shore
Cupping its palm
To drink up the sun
As though it was a swig of 'Joshanda'.
It remains healthy always
Never losing weight!
Sometimes it looks as though it is a magical island
This island of Mumbai . . .

Its sky is made of the skin of some chameleon
Changing colour as do promises
Revolving like a roulette in a casino!
This city is spinning forever
It has bearings attached to it
And is placed on some axle!

तिलस्मी शहर के मन्ज़र अजब हैं
अकेले रात को निकलो, सियाह साटिन की सड़कों पर
तिलस्मी चेहरे ऊपर जगमगाते 'होर्डिंग' पर झूलते हैं
सितारे झांकते हैं, नीचे सड़कों पर
वहां चढ़ने के जीने ढूंढ़ने पड़ते हैं
        पातालों में गुम हो कर

यहां जीना भी जादू है . . .
यहां पर ख़्वाब भी टांगों पे चलते हैं
उमंगें फूटती हैं, जिस तरह पानी में रखे मूंग के दाने
        चटख़ते हैं तो ज़ुबां उगने लगती है
यहां दिल ख़र्च हो जाते हैं अक्सर . . . कुछ नहीं बचता
सभी चाटे हुए पत्तल हवा में उड़ते रहते हैं
समन्दर रात को जब आंख बंद करता है, ये नगरी
पहन कर सारे ज़ेवर आसमां पर अक्स अपना देखा करती है

कभी 'सिंदबाद' भी आया तो होगा इस जज़ीरे पर
ये आधी पानी और आधी ज़मीं पर, ज़िन्दा मछली
        देख कर, हैरां हुआ होगा!!

The scenes of this magical city are strange.
If you come out alone at night
On its satin black roads
Enchanting faces sway from hoardings on top
Stars peep down on the roads below
To reach them you need to look for stairs going above
By losing yourself in the underworlds below.

To live here is like magic . . .
Even dreams here walk on feet
Hope breaks out just like seeds kept in water
Sprout and begin to grow tongues
Hearts often spend themselves out here . . . with
        nothing left
Swaying in the wind like leaf-plates licked clean
When the ocean shuts its eyes at night
This city, wearing all its ornaments,
Keeps looking at its reflection in the sky.

Sindbad too must have come sometime to this island
He must have been surprised to see this live fish
Half in the water and half on the ground!

न्यूयॉर्क

तुम्हारे शहर में ऐ दोस्त क्यों कर च्यूंटियों के घर नहीं हैं
कहीं भी च्यूंटियां देखीं नहीं मैंने
अगरचे फ़र्श पर चीनी भी डाली,
     पर कोई च्यूंटी नहीं आई
हमारे गांव के घर में तो आटा डालते हैं, गर
     क़तार उनकी नज़र आये

तुम्हारे शहर में गरचे . . .
     बहुत सब्ज़ा है, कितने ख़ूबसूरत पेड़ हैं
     पौदे हैं, फूलों से भरे हैं
कोई भंवरा मगर देखा नहीं भंवराये उन पर
तुम्हारे हां तो दीवारों में सीलन भी नहीं है
दरारें ही नहीं पड़तीं
हमारे यहां तो दस दिन के लिये परनाला गिरता है,
     तो उस दीवार से पीपल की डाली (कोंपल) फूट पड़ती है

ग़रीबी की मुझे आदत पड़ी है, या मैं तुम पर रश्क करता हूं . . .
तुम्हारे शहर की नक़लें हमारे हां महानगरों में होने लग गई हैं
मगर कमबख़्त आबादी बड़ी बरसाती होती है

यहां न्यूयॉर्क में कीड़े–मकोड़ों की कभी नस्लें नहीं बढ़तीं
सड़क पर गर्द भी उड़ती नहीं देखी–

New York

In your town, my friend, how is it that there are no
    homes for ants?
Nowhere could I see ants
Even when I put sugar on the floor
No ant came forward.
In our village home we put some dough
If we see a line of ants!

In your town although there is so much greenery
Beautiful trees, plants, and so many flowers
I never saw a swarm of bees hovering over them
Even your walls are never damp
That is why no peepal shoots break out from them:
Your walls never have any crevices!
Either I am used to poverty or I am envious of you . . .
We too need to build towns like you!

In your town, the lineage of insects and spiders never
    grow
Nor can one ever see dust swirling on the roads.

मेरा गांव बड़ा पिछड़ा हुआ है
मेरे आंगन के बरगद पर
सुबह कितनी तरह के पंछी आते हैं
वो नालायक़, वहीं खाते हैं दाना, और वहीं पर बीट करते हैं

तुम्हारे शहर में कुछ रोज़ रह लूं तो–
तो अपना गांव हिंदुस्तान मुझको याद आता है!

My village is so backward
At dawn, in the banyan in my courtyard,
So many kinds of birds come
The imbeciles, they both eat and shit there!

If I get to stay in your town for a few days
I miss my village India.

दिल्ली की दोपहर

सन्नाटों में लिपटी वो दोपहर कहां अब
धूप में आधी रात का सन्नाटा रहता था

लू से झुलसी दिल्ली की दोपहर में अक्सर . . .
'चारपाई' बुनने वाला जब
घंटाघर वाले नुक्कड़ से, कान पे रख के हाथ, इक हांक लगाता था
'चार . . . पाई . . . बुनवा लो . . .!'
ख़सख़स की टटियों में सोये लोग अन्दाज़ा कर लेते थे . . .
डेढ़ बजा है

दो बजते—बजते जामुन वाला गुज़रेगा
'जामुन . . . ठंडे . . . काले . . . जामुन...'
टोकरी में बड़ के पत्तों पर पानी छिड़क के रखता था
बंद कमरों में . . .
बच्चे कानी आंख से लेटे—लेटे मां को देखते थे,
      वो करवट लेकर सो जाती थी

तीन बजे तक लू का सन्नाटा रहता था
चार बजे तक 'लंगरी सोटा' पीसने लगता था ठंडाई
चार बजे के पास—पास ही हापड़ के पापड़ आते थे

Afternoon in Delhi

Where now are those hushed afternoons
When in bright sunshine there used to be the silence of
    midnight?

Often, in the 'loo'-scorched afternoons of Delhi,
The man who made charpais
Would stand at the corner of Ghanta Ghar
And with his hand on his ears
Let out the call:
'Get . . . your . . . charpais . . . made'
Those sleeping behind khus-cooled screens
Would know then: it must be half past one.

Around two, the jamun man would pass by:
'Cool . . . jamuns . . . black . . . jamuns'
He would keep them inside a basket
On barh leaves sprinkled with water;
Inside closed rooms
Children with one eye open
Would look at their mothers
And she would take a turn
And go to sleep again.

Till about three the loo-imposed stillness would remain
Around four, 'Langri Sota' would begin to grind the
    thandayi;
At about the same time the papads from Hapad would
    arrive:

'लो . . . हापड़ . . . के . . . पापड़ . . .'
लू की कन्नी टूटने पर छिड़काव होता था
आंगन और दुकानों पर

बर्फ़ की सिल पर सजने लगती थीं गंडेरियां
केवड़ा छिड़का जाता था
और छतों पर बिस्तर लग जाते थे जब
ठन्डे–ठन्डे आसमान पर
तारे छटकने लगते थे!

'Enjoy . . . the . . . papads . . . of . . . Hapad'
When the loo subsided, water was sprinkled
Outside shops and in courtyards;
Sugar cane pieces would now adorn slabs of ice
Kewda fragrance would be sprinkled;
And when on rooftops the beds would be made
Stars would twinkle
In the cool sky above.

कलकत्ता

कभी देखा है बिल्डिंग में, किसी सीढ़ी के नीचे
जहां मीटर लगे रहते हैं बिजली के
पुराने ज़ंग आलूदा . . .
खुले ढक्कन के नीचे पान खाये मैले दांतों की तरह
      कुछ फ्युज़ वाली प्लेट्स रखी हैं
पुराने पेच, मेख़ें जो निकाली थीं, वहीं रखी हैं कोने में
कई रंगों की तारों के सिरे जोड़े हुए सीढ़ी के नीचे,
      ठोक कर कीलें,
कई धागों से बांधे होल्डर पर, बल्ब नंगा झूलता है
      बेहया बदमाश लड़के की तरह जो
      खिलखिला के हंसता रहता है!

बहुत कटती हैं तारें, फ्युज़ उड़ते हैं
मगर बत्ती हमेशा जलती रहती है
ये कलकत्ता है कलकत्ता!
बहर सूरत हमेशा ज़िन्दा रहता है!!

82

Kolkata

Have you ever seen
Under the stairs of some building,
Where electric meters are installed,
Old rusted fuse plates
Sitting like paan-stained teeth
Inside an open box?
Old screws, pulled-out nails, lie in a corner
And, from under those very stairs,
Wires of many colours
Joined to each other
Stretch out from nails hammered into the wall.
A naked bulb
Somehow tied to the wires
Sways in the wind
Like the laughter
Of an unrepentant boy.

Wires are cut very often, fuses go off
But the lights are always on:
This is Kolkata, Kolkata!
Whatever happens, it is always alive!

ख़ाली पड़ा है ये मकान, मुद्दतें हुईं

ख़ाली पड़ा है ये मकान, मुद्दतें हुईं
ऊपर खुला दरीचा है, जिससे कभी–कभी
कुछ धूप आया करती है, फिर लौट जाती है

बाहर से आते–जाते हवा भी कभी–कभी
दरवाज़ा खटखटा के इन्तेज़ार करती है . . .
अब घर में कोई हो तो उठे, कुंडी खोल दे

हां बारिशों में जब कभी बादल गरजते हैं
इक टॉर्च जलती–बुझती है, ऊपर दरीचे में
लगता है कोई झांक रहा है मकान में

बूढ़े से एक अब्र की आवाज़ आती है
'ये मुश्ते–ख़ाक, छोड़ भी, कब तक संभालेगा?
बाहर एक आसमान तुझे लेने आया है!'

This Empty House

For ages now this house has been empty
Upstairs there is an open window through which
Off and on the sun peeps in and returns.

The wind wafts in sometimes from outside
And knocks on the door, waiting,
Someone inside may get up and open the lock.

Yes, in the monsoons when the clouds at times thunder
A torch blinks in the window above
It seems that someone is peering inside.

A voice from an aging cloud resounds:
'Leave this mortal clay, how long will you nurture it?
Outside, the sky has come to take you away.'

नाव में बहते–बहते . . .

नाव में बहते–बहते इक नज़्म मेरी पानी में गिरी और गलने लगी
काग़ज़ का पैराहन था
मेरी तहरीर न थाम सका

सियाही फैल गई पहले
फिर लफ़्ज़ गले, और एक–एक कर के डूब गये
टूटते मिसरों की हिचकी, कुछ दूर सुनाई दी और फिर . . .
बाक़ीमांदा . . .
कुछ मानी थे
कुछ देर किसी तलछट की तरह
पानी की सतह पर तैरे और फिर बहते–बहते,
    आंख से ओझल होते गये!

Floating Boat

From a boat floating along
A poem of mine fell in the water
And began to dissolve;
It wore the garment of paper
Which could not hold my verses.

First, the ink spread;
Then the words dissolved and, one by one, drowned
The sobs of breaking verses could be heard from some
    distance
And then, everything faded
Some meanings, like scum,
Floated awhile on the surface of the water
And then disappeared from sight!

मुझे मेरा जिस्म छोड़ कर बह गया नदी में

मुझे मेरा जिस्म छोड़ कर बह गया नदी में
अभी उसी दिन की बात है मैं नहाने उतरा था घाट पर जब
ठिठर रहा था . . .
वो छू के पानी की सर्द तहज़ीब, डर गया था

मैं सोचता था
बगैर मेरे वो कैसे काटेगा तेज़ धारा
वो बहते पानी की बेरुख़ी जानता नहीं है
वो डूब जायेगा . . . सोचता था

अब उस किनारे पहुंच के मुझको बुला रहा है
मैं इस किनारे पे डूबता जा रहा हूं पैहम
मैं कैसे तैरूं बगैर उसके!

मुझे मेरा जिस्म छोड़ के बह गया नदी में!!

My Body Left Me and Flowed Away
with the River

My body has left me and flowed away with the river!
Just the other day when I had gone down to the ghat
    for a bath
My body was shivering . . .
Touching the water's frigid nature, it was frightened.

I used to think:
Without me how will it negotiate the fast currents
It does not know the indifference of flowing waters
It will drown . . . so I used to think.

Now, having reached the other shore it calls out to me
While here, on this shore, I keep drowning constantly:
How can I swim without my body?

My body has left me and flowed away with the river!

तुम गये तो और कुछ नहीं हुआ . . .

तुम गये तो और कुछ नहीं हुआ
दिल पे ऐतमाद घट गया मेरा
मैं जो दिल के पीछे, उसके नक़्शे—पा पे
        पांव रखके चलता था
चलते—चलते देखा तो निशान ख़त्म हो गये
तुम गये तो और कुछ नहीं हुआ
दिल से ऐतबार उठ गया मेरा!!

When You Left Nothing Else Happened

When you left nothing else happened
Except that
My reliance on my heart reduced.
In the past
I used to trace His footsteps
Step by step.
Then, walking along, I noticed
The imprint of the footsteps had vanished.

When you left nothing else happened
Except that my faith in my heart was no more.

धूप लगे आकाश पे जब

धूप लगे आकाश पे जब
दिन में चांद नज़र आया था
डाक से आया मुहर लगा
एक पुराना सा तेरा, चिट्ठी का लिफ़ाफ़ा याद आया
चिट्ठी गुम हुये तो अरसा बीत चुका
मुहर लगा, बस मटियाला सा
उसका लिफ़ाफ़ा रखा है!

When the Sun Touched the Sky

In the sunny sky
I saw the moon during the day
An old envelope of a letter from you
Delivered by post, with the stamped seal,
Came to mind
The letter has been lost for ages
The envelope, muddy-looking,
With the stamped seal
Remains.

सब कुछ वैसे ही चलता है

सब कुछ वैसे ही चलता है
जैसे चलता था जब तुम थीं
रात भी वैसे ही सर मूंदे आती है
दिन वैसे ही आंखें मलता जागता है
तारे सारी रात जमाइयां लेते हैं
सब कुछ वैसे ही चलता है, जैसे चलता था जब तुम थीं

काश तुम्हारे जाने पर
कुछ फ़र्क़ तो पड़ता जीने में
प्यास न लगती पानी की या नाख़ुन बढ़ना बंद हो जाते
बाल हवा में न उड़ते या धुआं निकलता सांसों से
सब कुछ वैसे ही चलता है . . .

बस इतना फ़र्क़ पड़ा है मेरी रातों में
नींद नहीं आती तो अब सोने के लिये
इक नींद की गोली रोज़ निगलनी पड़ती है!

Everything Goes On as Before

Everything goes on, exactly as it used to
When you were there:
The night still comes with its head drooping
The day too dawns still rubbing its eyes
All night the stars yawn
Everything goes on exactly as it used to
When you were there.

I wish after you had left
Something would have changed in my life:
I would not feel thirsty, or my nails would stop
    growing
My hair would no longer fly in the wind
Or smoke would come out of my nostrils
But, everything goes on as before.

Only there is a change in my nights:
I cannot sleep, and to do so
I have to swallow a sleeping tablet daily!

खूबानी, अखरोट . . .

खूबानी, अखरोट बहुत दिन पास रहे थे
दोनों के जब अक्स पड़ा करते थे बहते दरिया में
पेड़ों की पोशकें छोड़ के
नंग–धड़ंग दोनों दिन भर पानी में तैरा करते थे
कभी–कभी तो पार का छोर भी छू आते थे

खूबानी मोटी थी और अखरोट का क़द कुछ ऊंचा था
भंवर कोई पीछे पड़ जाये, तो पत्थर की आड़ से होकर
अखरोट का हाथ पकड़ के वापस भाग आती थी

अखरोट बहुत समझाता था
'देख खुबानी, भंवर के चक्कर में मत पड़ना,
पांव तले की मिट्टी खींच लिया करता है!'

इक शाम बहुत पानी आया तुग़ियानी का
और एक भंवर–
खूबानी को पांव से उठाकर, तुग़ियानी में कूद गया

अखरोट अब भी उस जानिब देखा करता है, जिस जानिब दरया
   बहता है
अखरोट का क़द कुछ सहम गया है
उसका अक्स नहीं पड़ता अब पानी में!

Apricot, Walnut

An apricot and a walnut stood for long close together;
When their shadows fell in the flowing river
They shed their clothes
And swam the whole day stark naked
Sometimes going as far as the other shore.

The apricot was a little plump, the walnut a little taller
If a whirlpool chased her
The apricot would take the support of a boulder
And escape catching hold of the walnut's hand.

The walnut would try to make her understand:
'Listen, Apricot, don't get entangled with that
        whirlpool
It drags the ground from under your feet.'

One evening, the river was in spate
And a whirlpool
Lifting the apricot by her feet
Jumped into the raging waters.

The walnut still gazes in the direction the river flows
His height has slightly shrunk
Now his shadow does not reflect in the water.

पीपल . . .

कितना कूड़ा करता है पीपल आंगन में
मां को दिन में दो बार बोहारी फेरनी पड़ती है

कैसे—कैसे दोस्त—यार आते हैं इसके
खाने को ये पीपलियां देता है
सारा दिन शाख़ों पे बैठे तोते, घुग्घु
आधा खाते, आधा ज़ाया करते हैं
गिटक—विटक सब आंगन ही में फेंक के जाते हैं

एक डाल पर, चिड़ियों ने भी घर बांधे हैं
तिनके उड़ते रहते हैं दिन भर आंगन में
एक गिलहरी भोर से लेकर सांझ तलक
जाने क्या उजलत रहती है—
दौड़—दौड़ कर दसियों बार ही सारी शाख़ें घूम आती है
चील कभी ऊपर की डारी पर बैठी, बौराई सी
अपने आप से बातें करती रहती है

आस—पड़ोस से झप्टी, लूटी, हड्डी, मांस की बोटी भी कमबख़्त
    ये कव्वे
पीपल ही की डाल पे बैठ के खाते हैं
ऊपर से कहता है पीपल, पक्का बिरहमन है
हुश—हुश करती है मां तो ये मांसख़ोर सब
काएं—काएं उस पर फेंक के उड़ जाते हैं
फिर भी जाने क्यों मां कहती है: 'आ कागा . . .
'मेरे श्राध पे आयो तू! आवश्य आयो!'

Peepal

How much muck this peepal creates in the courtyard
Mother has to wield the broom twice a day.

To all kinds of friends who come visiting
It offers seedlings
Parrots and pigeons, sitting on its branches the
　　whole day,
Eat some, waste more
Throwing the kernels
In this very courtyard before leaving.

Birds too have built their nests on a branch
Twigs fly around the courtyard all the time
From dawn to dusk a squirrel—
God knows what the hurry is—
Runs incessantly up and down every branch
An eagle, seated on a higher branch, like someone
　　insane,
Keeps talking to itself.

These damned crows also eat the bones and flesh
Snatched or looted from the neighbourhood
On the branches of this very tree
To mother's cries of 'hoosh-hoosh'
They fly away cackling
Dropping their carnivorous fare on her.
Even so, who knows why, Mother always says:
O crow, when my sraddh is held, come, do come!

इमली . . .

कोसबाद के नुक्कड़ पर
इक मुस्टन्डा पेड़ खड़ा है, इमली का
उसका गुस्सा नहीं उतरता
अदरक जैसी मोटी—मोटी गिरहें पड़ी हैं जोड़ों में
सारा दिन खुजलाता है, एक्ज़ीमा है

जिस मोड़ पे है, उस मोड़ पे जब बस रुकती है
जल्दी—जल्दी, बीड़ी बुझा कर उसके बदन पर
लोग बसों में चढ़ जाते हैं
पान की पीक भी थूक दिया करते हैं उस पर
चक्कू से काटे हैं लोगों ने उसकी शाख़ों के डन्ठल
खड़े—ख़ड़े बस यूंही उस पर ढेले फेंका करते हैं
इसी लिए तो उसका गुस्सा नहीं उतरता

भूरे लाल मकोड़ों को
ज़िंदा ही निगल जाता है अक्सर
बांह झटक के नीचे फेंक दिया करता है
अड्डी—टप्पा खेलती गोल गिलहरी को
च्यूंटियां पाल रखी हैं उसने
टेक लगाये कोई, या कोई जूता झाड़े उस पर तो . . .
च्यूंटियां छोड़ दिया करता है

उसका गुस्सा नहीं उतरता है
कोसबाद के नुक्कड़ पर
इक मुस्टन्डा पेड़ खड़ा है, इमली का!!

Imli

In Kosbad, at the crossing,
Stands a stout imli tree
That never ceases to be angry.
Thick knots, like on a ginger root, plague his joints
All day he scratches himself, he has eczema.

At the turn where he stands
When buses stop
People hurriedly stub their bidis on his body
Before they board
They spit out paan spittle on him too
People have used knives to cut his twigs
Thrown stones at him, just like that, while idling around
That is why he never ceases to be angry!

Often he swallows up live red and brown spiders
Or jerks his hands to throw to the ground
A playful squirrel
He has ants as pets
If someone leans against him
Or uses him to clean their shoes
The ants are unleashed.

His anger never ceases
In Kosbad, at the crossing,
Stands a robust imli tree!

हमें पेड़ों की पोशाकों से इतनी सी ख़बर तो मिल ही जाती है

हमें पेड़ों की पोशकों से इतनी सी ख़बर तो मिल ही जाती है
बदलने वाला है मौसम . . .!
नये आवेज़े कानों में लटकते देख कर कोयल ख़बर देती है
    बारी आम की आई . . .!
कि बस अब मौसम–ए–गर्मा शुरू होगा
सभी पत्ते गिरा के गुलमोहर जब नंगा हो जाता है गर्मी में
तो ज़र्दा–सुर्ख़, सब्ज़े पर छपी, पोशाक की तैयारी करता है
पता चलता है कि बादल की आमद है

पहाड़ों से पिघलती बर्फ़ बहती है धुलाने पैर 'पाइन' के
हवाएं झाड़ के पत्ते उन्हें चमकाने लगती हैं

मगर जब रेंगने लगती है इन्सानों की बस्ती
हरी पगडन्डियों के पांव जब बाहर निकलते हैं
समझ जाते हैं सारे पेड़, अब कटने की बारी आ रही है
यही बस आख़री मौसम है जीने का, इसे जी लो!

The Garments of Trees

From what the trees are wearing, at least this we learn:
The season is about to change . . .!
Seeing new adornments hanging from ears
The koyal gives the news:
It's time for the mango season . . .!

Any moment now summer will begin;
Shedding all its leaves, when the gulmohar stands nude
    in summer,
Preparing to wear a dress of red and gold stamped on green
One knows that clouds are about to come.

When the melting snows flow to wash the feet of the pine
The winds brush off its leaves and begin to polish them.

But when human settlements begin to slither
And green pathways begin to walk out of them
All the trees understand, the time has come for us to be cut
This is the last season to live, live it fully!

लम्हों पर बैठी नज़्मों को

लम्हों पर बैठी नज़्मों को
तितली जाल में बंद कर लेना
फिर, काट के पर उन नज़्मों को
अल्बम में 'पिन' करते रहना
ज़ुल्म नहीं तो और क्या है?

लम्हे काग़ज़ पर गिर के ममियाये जाते हैं
नज़्मों के रंग रह जाते हैं पोरों पर!!

A Poem Perched on a Moment

A poem perched on a moment
Imprisoned in a butterfly net
Then its wings cut off
To keep it pinned in an album:
If this is not injustice, what is?

Entangled in the paper the moments are mummified
Only the colours of the poem remain on my fingertips!

वो जो 'पब' है . . .

लस्सन की, और तम्बाकू की बू से भरा
नीची छत वाला जो 'पब' है
और जहां मौसीकी नंगी घूम रही है
उधड़ी–उधड़ी रौशनी, एड़ी पांव पटख़ के
      नाच रही है!

कच्चे मसाले, प्याज़, पसीना, और धुएं की
      लटकी–लटकी लपटों में . . .
ठन्डे से संगेमरमर की इक मैली मेज़ पे बैठा शायर
लहू में लिथड़ी 'आनोल नाड़' को काट रहा था
अभी–अभी इक नज़्म का जन्म हुआ है शायद!!

In That Pub

Reeking of tobacco and garlic
That pub with the low roof
Where music roams naked
And murky light dances
Stomping its feet . . .

Amidst the stench of
Raw spices, sweat and onions
And the heat of smoke hanging low
Sits a poet on a cold and dirty marbletop table
Severing an umbilical cord drenched in blood:
Perhaps, just now, a new poem has been born!

वो जो इक ख़्याल था

वो जो इक ख़्याल था
तेज़ धार की तरह
काटता गुज़र गया . . .
लहू के क़तरे–क़तरे से
उबल पड़े थे जिस्म पर

ठन्डा पड़ के, बूंद–बूंद, पानी बन के बह गया
सब्ज़े की तरह खिला हुआ है मेरी नज़्म पर!!

That One Thought

That one thought
Sharp like a razor's edge
Slashed its way past . . .
Scalding drops of blood
Came up all over my body.

On cooling, it became water and drop by drop flowed
    away
Now like verdure it has blossomed on my verse!

ऐश ट्रे पूरी भर गई है . . .

जगह नहीं और डायरी में
ये ऐश ट्रे पूरी भर गई है
भरी हुई है जले–बुझे अधकहे ख़्यालों की राखो–बू से
ख़्याल पूरी तरह से जो कि जले नहीं थे
मसल दिया या दबा दिया था, बुझे नहीं वो
कुछ उनके टुर्रें पड़े हुए हैं
बस एक–दो कश ही लेके कुछ मिसरे रह गये थे

कुछ ऐसी नज़्में जो तोड़ कर फेंक दी थीं उसमें
धुआं न निकले
कुछ ऐसे अशआर जो मेरे ब्रांड के नहीं थे
वो एक ही कश में खांस कर, ऐश ट्रे में
        घिस के बुझा दिये थे

इस ऐश ट्रे में
'ब्लेड' से काटी रात की नब्ज़ से टपकते
        सियाह क़तरे बुझे हुए हैं
छिले हुये चांद की क़ाशें
जो रात भर छील–छील कर फेंकता रहा हूं
घड़ी हुई पेन्सिलों के छिलके
ख़्यालों की शिद्दतों से जो टूटती रही हैं।

110

The Ash-tray Is Overflowing

No more place is left in the diary:
This ash-tray is completely full!
It is full of the ash and smell of
Half-lit, half-burnt, half-said thoughts;
Thoughts which were not yet fully alight
Stubbed or pushed away, not yet extinguished;
Only some remnants lying about
And some verses
From whom only one or two drags were taken.

Some poems broken and thrown in
So that they do not smoulder;
Other couplets, not of my brand,
Stubbed, after coughing on but one puff.

In this ash-tray
Lie extinguished black drops
Dripping from the vein of the night
Cut by a blade;
Slivers from the moon
Which I have scraped the whole night;
Shavings of pencils which
Kept breaking against the extremes of thought.

इस ऐश ट्रे में
हैं तीलियां कुछ कटे हुए नामों नम्बरों की
जलाई थीं चन्द नज़्में जिन से
धुआं अभी तक दियासलाई से झड़ रहा है
उलट–पलट के तमाम सफ़हों में झांकता हूं
कहीं कोई टुर्रा नज़्म का बच गया हो तो उसका कश लगा लूं
तलब लगी है
ये ऐश ट्रे पूरी भर गई है!!

In this ash-tray
Are matchsticks of some scratched out names and
    numbers;
Once these had ignited a few poems
Smoke still hangs around them;
I peep into all the pages,
Turning them up and down
To see if there is any stub of a poem left
On which I can take a puff;
The urge is still there!
But this ash-tray is completely full.

इक नज़्म का मिसरा कसते हुए

इक नज़्म का मिसरा कसते हुए
अल्फ़ाज़ के जंगल में घुस कर
मख़्सूस कोई मानी जब तोड़ के लाता हूं
हाथों पे ख़राशें पड़ती हैं
और उंगलियां छिल जाती हैं मगर
वो लफ़्ज़ जुबां पे रखते ही
मुंह में इक रस घुल जाता है!

A Line in a Verse

While composing a line of a poem
When I am able to penetrate the jungle of words
And break off a special meaning
My hands are scratched
And my fingers bruised
But
The moment that word is on my tongue
A relish dissolves in my mouth!

सरदार डैम

तीन पहाड़ों बीच बनी इस वादी में
बंध बनेगा!
डैम बनेगा!

सर पर लो, और चलो उठालो, छाबा खोंचा इस गांव का
रिश्ते–नाते, आस–पड़ोस, अब सब रेढ़ी पर रखो और लुढ़काओ उनको
झल्ली में डालो मिट्टी पिछली पुश्तों की, और माज़ी कन्धे पे रखलो
जेब में भर लो क़ब्रें अपनी
रीत–रिवाज और कल्चर–वल्चर, गर्दन में लटका के उठो
कमर पे बांधो नंगे बच्चे . . .
पीपल, तुलसी, मढ़ी–वढ़ी, दरगाहें, मीठे कुएं, चलो सब औंधे कर दो
कूच करो अब!

तीन पहाड़ों में से रेंगता, बल खाता जो सदियों से बहता आया है
कुन्डली मार के बैठेगा वो दरिया अब इस वादी में!

116

Sardar Dam

In this valley cradled between three mountains
A dam will be built!
A dam will be built!

Come, load on your head and haul away
The bits and pieces of this village
Pile your kinships and relationships onto a cart
And topple them away
Shove the dust of earlier generations into a basket
Carry the past on your shoulder
And stuff family tombs into your pocket
Customs, rituals and such things like culture
Hang around your neck before you leave
Around your waist tie naked children . . .
Peepal, tulsi, shrines, memorials, sweet water wells . . .
Come, upend them all
And just decamp!

That river which for ages
Has come cascading down
Between three mountains
Will now sit coiled like a snake
In this valley!

सामने वाली उस पहाड़ी पर

सामने वाली उस पहाड़ी पर
वो जो भूरी चट्टान दिखती है
एक तंदुरुस्त पेड़ का साया
सुबह की धूप में आकर
हाथ–पांव पसार के हर रोज़
देर तक लेटा रहता था . . .
    काट के पेड़ ले गये कुछ लोग
    और साया पड़ा सिसकता रहा

जहां–जहां, चलाया था आरा
जहां–जहां लगी थी कुल्हाड़ी
उसके ज़ख़्मों से खून बहता रहा

अब भी भूरी चट्टान पर खूं के
काले–काले से दाग़ मिलते हैं!

On the Mountain Opposite

That tan cliff that you can see
On the mountain opposite:
A shadow of a healthy tree
With the help of the morning sun
Used to lie there every day for long,
Its hands and feet spread out.

Some people cut the tree and took it away:
The shadow, whimpering, was left behind.

Wherever the saw was used
Wherever the axe was wielded
Blood flows from its wounds.

Even now, on that tan mountain,
Blackish spots of blood can be found.

नौ साला फ़राज़ का कहना है . . .

बड़ा होने लगा था, फिर ख़याल आया
कि रुक जाऊं . . .
जो पानी पी रहा हूं मैं, वो गदला है
हवा भी बासी लगती है . . .!
सड़क पे छांव रहती थी
उसे भी टुकड़ा–टुकड़ा काट के सब ले गये कब के
मैं घर आया तो टी.वी. में धुआं देखा
कहीं पे ट्रेन जलती थी
किसी ने बस जला दी थी
घरों को जलते–गिरते देख कर घर से निकल आया

अगर आधी सदी से, आप ही कहिये
यही सब चल रहा है तो
इसी में आपका बचपन गया होगा
इसी में मैं बड़ा हूंगा
तो फिर कितना ज़रूरी है बड़ा होना!

As I Began to Grow Up

As I began to grow up, a thought came to me
That I should do so no more . . .
The water that I drink is muddy
The air too appears stale
The shade that used to caress the road
Has also been hacked, piece by piece,
And taken away by people long ago!
When I returned home I saw smoke on the TV screen
Somewhere a train was burning
Someone had burnt a bus
Watching homes being burnt or demolished
I came out of my home.

If for half a century
Such things have been going on
And your childhood has been exposed to it
And so must mine
Then, how necessary is it to grow up?

नंग–धड़ंग ज़मीं पर लेटे–लेटे मैंने

नंग–धड़ंग ज़मीं पर लेटे–लेटे मैंने
कितनी बार सुना है इस मिट्टी के नीचे
कुछ आवाज़ें रेंग रही हैं

कान लगा कर, दरियाओं के छुप जाने की चाप सुनी है,
छोटे–छोटे बीजों के फटने से अन्दर . . .
पेड़ों के गिरने की सी भारी आवाज़ें गूंजती हैं
औलादों को घर के बाहर जाने से कोई रोक रहा है
ऊपर मत जान कि . . .
लोग ज़मीं के कपड़े, लत्ते, ज़ेवर, नोच–नोच कर बेच रहे हैं
ज़मीं की दुल्हन लूट रहे हैं
चीर हरण का दौर चला है!!

122

Lying on the Naked Ground

Lying on the naked ground
How many times have I heard
Some voices slithering below the soil.

Straining my ear I have heard
The stress of rivers forced to go into hiding
Even in the sprouting below of the smallest seeds
There echoes the cry akin to falling trees
Someone is trying to stop their children from leaving home
Don't go up:
Because people are tearing off
The attire and ornaments and everything else
Of the earth
To put them to sale!
They are plundering this bride-like earth:
The scene of Draupadi's stripping is on!

कुछ दिन पहले . . .

कुछ दिन पहले . . .
पाकिस्तान में बाबा रहते थे
लाहौर बड़ा अपना लगता था
आख़री बार आवाज़ सुनी थी बाबा की
'गर्मी है, इस बारिश हो जाये तो ठीक हो जायेगा
सांस दमे में घुटने लगती है!'
सांस ही तोड़ दी बाबा ने
कोई नहीं अब शहर में अपना
लाहौर अब सिर्फ़ पड़ोसी है!!

Some Days Ago

Some time ago
Baba* used to live in Pakistan;
Lahore seemed to be part of my self.
The last time I heard his voice, he said:
'Its hot, one rain and all will be well
Its so suffocating to breathe with this asthma.'
But Baba, you gave up the breath!
Now no one is my own in the city
Lahore is now only a neighbour!

*The celebrated Urdu poet Ahmed Nadim Qasimi

बाबा

जब चिराग़ बुझता है
इक धुआं सा उठता है
आफ़ताब शाम को
जब ग़ुरूब होता है
टीन का फ़लक भी तो
देर तक सुलगता है
पत्ते टूटते हैं तो
थोड़ी दूर उड़ते हैं
तुमने जाते वक़्त क्यों
मुड़ के देखा भी नहीं
सांस रोकी और तुम
मिट्टी ओढ़ सो गये!

Baba

When a candle dies
Some form of smoke rises;
At dusk
When the sun goes down
This tin-like sky also
Smoulders for long;
When leaves break
They too float in the air for a distance.
Why then did you
At the time of leaving
Not look back even once?
You just stopped your breath
Took the earth as a cover
And went to sleep.

एक ख़्याल को काग़ज़ पर दफ़नाया तो

एक ख़्याल को काग़ज़ पर दफ़नाया तो
इक नज़्म ने आंखें खोल के देखा
ढेरों लफ़्ज़ों के नीचे वो दबी हुई थी

सहमी सी, इक मद्धम सी, आवाज़ की भाप
    उड़ी कानों तक
क्यों इतने लफ़्ज़ों में मुझको चुनते हो?
बाहें कस दी हैं मिसरों की
तशबीहों के पर्दे में हर जुंबिश तह कर देते हो

इतनी ईंटें लगती हैं क्या एक ख़्याल दफ़नाने में?!

128

When a Thought Was Buried on Paper

When a thought was buried on paper
A poem opened its eyes and saw
Under how many mounds of words she was interred.

A voice like vapour, a bit withdrawn, not loud
Wafted by my ear:
Why do you brick me in with so many words?
The embrace of verses has been made so tight
You fold away my every movement within the veil
    of similes.

Do you need so many bricks to bury a thought?

उस कलसी का पेंदा नहीं है

उस कलसी का पेंदा नहीं है
जिस कलसी को दरिया में हर रोज़ डुबो कर
पानी भर के लाता हूं
और अपनी क्यारियां सींचता हूं

पेंदा नहीं है उस लोटे का—
जिस लोटे से गंगा घाट पे बैठ के रोज़ नहाता हूं
और खुश्क बदन को पोंछ के मैं, पोशाक बदल लेता हूं

बिन पेंदे के डोल से मैं
रोज़ कुएं से पानी खींच के
बाक़ी बर्तन भरने की कोशिश करता हूं
सब भांडे प्यासे रहते हैं

बिन पेंदा हैं नाम खुदा के
उनमें अब ईमान नहीं भरता!!

Kalsi

That pitcher which I dip
In the river every day
To water my plants
Has no base.

This mug
Which I use every day
To have a bath seated on the ghat of the Ganges
And wipe my body dry to change my clothes . . .
This too does not have a base.

The vessel with which
I pull out water from the well every day
To try and fill up other utensils
Is also without a base:
All the containers remain thirsty.

Base-less are the names of God
No longer can they be filled up with reverence or faith!

वो जो इक मीयाद थी ना

वो जो इक मीयाद थी ना
इस्तेमाल की—
वो गुज़र चुकी!!
दवा की शीशियों पे लिखी जाती है इसी लिए
मीयाद बाद इस्तमाल करने से
दवाइयां भी बासी होने लगती हैं
फिर कोई इलाज कर नहीं पातीं (सकतीं)
फिर भी तर्क न हुईं तो ज़हर बनने लगती हैं

बासी हो चुके मज़हबों के ए'तक़ाद सब—
वो जो इक मीयाद थी ना, इस्तमाल की
वो गुज़र चुकी!!

The 'Use By' Date

You know,
That 'use by' date . . .
That date has expired
It is written on medicine bottles only because
Once that date is over
Even medicines putrefy.
Then they cannot cure
And if still not abandoned
They become poison.

All the values that animated religions
Have putrefied
That 'use by' date that we spoke of . . .
That date has expired!